Let's travel in

ITALY

Edited by Darlene Geis

A TRAVEL PRESS BOOK

PICTURE ACKNOWLEDGMENTS
The full-color illustrations in this book are the work of the following photographers and artists whose collaboration is gratefully acknowledged. Photographed in Italy by Ace Williams (2, 3, 5, 6, 7, 11, 12, 20, 21, 22, 25, 29, 30, 32); Bernard Silberstein, from Rapho-Guillumette (4, 15); Robert Emmett Bright, from Rapho-Guillumette (9, 10); Federico Patellani, from P.I.P. (14, 16, 18); P.I.P. (31); Fritz Henle, from Photo Researchers (24, 27); D. Edwards, from F.P.G. (13, 28); David Seymour, from Magnum (17); Camera Clix (23); Shostal (26); Wolfe Worldwide Films (1); Three Lions (8, 19). For the black-and-white photographs we wish to thank Photo Researchers, Inc., Three Lions, Ace Williams, Orville Goldner, the Italian State Tourist Office, Dr. Sterling Wheelwright, P.I.P., and Wide World Photos. The map was made by Enrico Arno. Designed by Mann Associates.

CONTENTS

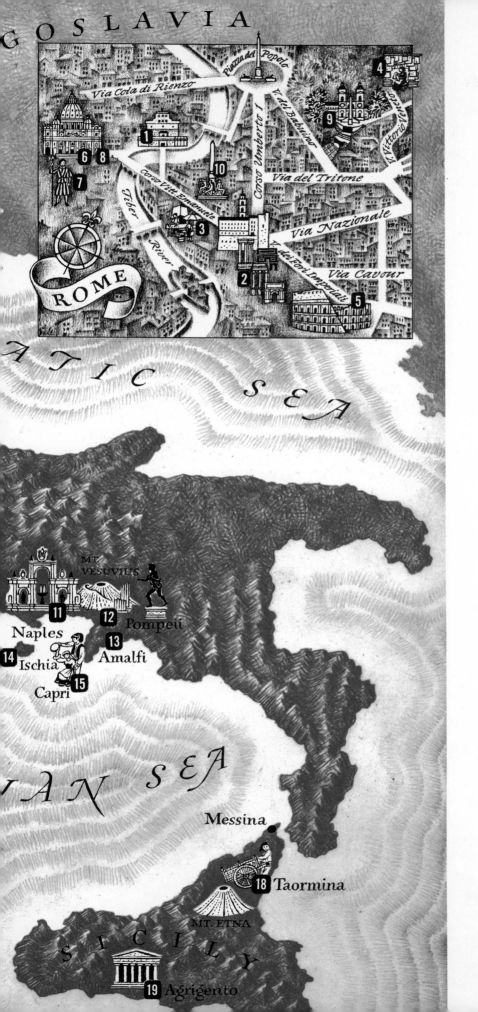

Locales of thirty-two full-page pictures

ITALY:

land of legendary beauty

THRUSTING down toward the warm Mediterranean Sea, the Italian peninsula is easily recognizable on any map of Europe. Its familiar shape is like a cavalier's boot with a flaring top, arched instep and high heel. The boot is pulled back as if for a well-aimed kick at the island of Sicily, which lies close to its toe. Walled away from the rest of Europe by a semicircle of jagged Alpine peaks to the north, the fair land of Italy stretches about 700 miles southward between the Adriatic and Tyrrhenian (*tih-*REE-*nih-an*) seas. From top to toe this long, thin country is a scenic delight. Just south of the Alps are narrow, blue mountain lakes—Maggiore (*mahd-*JOE-*ray*), Como and Garda—reflecting the clear Italian skies. Below them, from its source in the mountains to the west, the Po River flows eastward to the Adriatic through a fertile green valley. Here are vine-covered hills, orchards, and rich fields of corn and grain nodding beneath the sun.

South of the Po Valley, the great range of the Apennines (APP-*eh-nines*) comes in from the west, runs down the center of the boot to its very toe and then continues through Sicily. The hills that ripple out from this central ridge—sometimes all the way to the seacoast—are responsible for much of Italy's scenic grandeur. And since the peninsula is so long, it has miles and miles of shore line bathed by mild and azure seas. The western side in particular is remarkable for the picturesque villages and eye-filling beauty of its winding coast line.

9

WEALTH PAST COUNTING

Though richly endowed with beauty, Italy is a poor country. The land on which one can feast one's eyes is not always capable of producing food. Nearly 78 per cent of Italy's surface is mountainous and hilly, making cultivation difficult. Yet, thanks to the skill and hard work of her peasants, Italy resembles a vast garden where each little plot of ground has been diligently and lovingly tended. Her fruits, vegetables and flowers are superior in quality if not in quantity to those of other countries. Little oil and few metals are to be found beneath the surface of this beautiful land; Italy must send to other countries for those vital products. But if her wealth does not exist in a raw state deep within the earth, she has treasures beyond calculating in her magnificent cities and ancient towns. In a way, Italy is the custodian of the cultural wealth of the whole Western world. We who travel there come to share in her spiritual and artistic riches.

THE ETERNAL CITY

There was a time when the Western world was ruled from one small city about midway up the shin of the Italian boot. Rome in those days was the center of a mighty empire. It had thrown a vast network of roads over much of the known world, and within that firm net it held the world captive. "All roads lead to Rome," was the old saying, but actually they radiated *from* the city like rays from the sun. Over them the Roman legions marched, bringing Roman laws, language and customs to light the farthest outposts of the empire. Fifteen centuries have passed since the fall of that empire, but now the roads leading to Rome are crowded with travelers on pilgrimage to the city whose influence spread so far.

The legend of Romulus and Remus and the old she-wolf is immortalized in this famous bronze.

Apart from its past splendors, still very much in evidence, Rome is a modern capital busily involved in twentieth-century affairs. It is also the headquarters of the Roman Catholic Church, whose Vatican City is an independent and sovereign state within Rome. No metropolis exists today whose buildings and monuments span so many years and so many civilizations. There are remains of Stone Age settlements, the arches and columns of the Caesars, the magnificent cathedrals and churches of early Christianity, Renaissance palaces, and smart new hotels, shops and apartment buildings. The Tiber River winds through this City of the Seven Hills, and visitors are awed at the thought of how much water has flowed between those banks since the days when the earliest shepherds tended their flocks here. The history of Rome, however, is not the history of Italy. Each city has had its own story and its own civilization, and each section of the country has developed differently. These separate and distinct pieces, joined together within the last hundred years, make up the fascinating mosaic that is Italy.

THE INDUSTRIAL NORTH

Climate and geography have combined to make northern Italy vigorous and productive. The mountain people along the French and Swiss Alpine borders are hardy and energetic, and seem more like their foreign neighbors than like their countrymen to the south. In Piedmont even the language sounds French rather than Italian. Milan (*mee*-LAHN) and Turin (TOO-*rin*) are the two great industrial cities of Italy. Their factories get power from the torrential streams that rush down the mountainsides and into the Po Valley. This hydroelectric power has been called Italy's "white coal." Genoa, on the northwestern coast, is Italy's largest seaport. Today the Italian merchant marine ranks sixth in the world, and the Genoese sail the distant sea routes under the green, white and red flag of Italy. Genoa's opposite number on the northeastern coast is the Queen of the Adriatic, Venice. But Venice, like Rome, has its own unique story and background. It is a country unto itself.

11

The farmlands of the Po Valley are the most fertile in Italy. Here farming has become an industry, with paid hands and machinery doing a large-scale job. In the nineteenth century rice was introduced as an ideal crop for the marshy flooded plains of the Po Valley. Rice is an important ingredient of north Italian cooking, and in this part of the country *risotto* (*ree-*SAWT*-toh*) takes the place of *pasta* (PAHS*-tah*), the spaghetti, macaroni and noodle dishes of the rest of Italy.

CENTRAL ITALY, TRIUMPH OF NATURE AND ART

After the Roman Empire crumbled under the waves of barbarian invasions in the fifth century, Italy endured more than three hundred years of darkness. Then in 800 a new empire was established with Charlemagne's coronation in Rome as Emperor of the West. The dark-

In southern Italy the grapes grow sweet. Life, though hard, is merry.

ness began to lift, and in the fourteenth century Italy began its glorious rebirth—the golden age of the Renaissance had come. There were many independently wealthy and powerful centers—Venice, Rome, Milan—but it was in central Italy that the Renaissance flowered most brilliantly. Tuscany, the province that includes Florence, Pisa (PEE*-zah*) and Siena (*see-*EH*-nah*), still retains its Renaissance flavor. There are festivals each year in the rich costumes of those golden days. And throughout central Italy the rolling hills and tranquil villages remind us of the painted landscapes of the great Italian masters.

The Marches are in central Italy along the Adriatic shores. The Franks first gave this section its name, which comes from the Germanic word meaning borders. The Marches have a gentle climate, cooled by sea breezes, and the land is a series of slopes and valleys dropping from the ridge of the Apennines to the Adriatic. Some of the loveliest little seashore resorts stretch along this strip of coast.

This part of Italy was originally populated by the Sabines (SAY*-bines*), an early agricultural people. The earliest settlers of Rome invited some of their Sabine neighbors to a festival of public games. While the games were going on, the hosts carried off the Sabine women, an act which involved them in a bitter war. But the women intervened between their new lords and their brothers and husbands. The Roman and Sabine kings were reconciled, and the two peoples were united at the foot of the Roman Capitol, a place that has remained sacred ever since. The Marches are still a frontier country, dividing northern Italy, with its European character, from southern Italy, with its Saracen and Greek background.

SOUTHERN ITALY, WARM AND SMILING LAND

Just above the ankle of the Italian boot we come to Naples on its blue curve of bay, with Mt. Vesuvius smoking placidly in the background. Naples—and much of the land to the south, including the island of Sicily —was settled over 2,500 years ago by seafarers from Greece who called these colonies "greater Greece." There are ruins of Greek temples and theaters scattered throughout the foot of Italy and Sicily that are in a better state of preservation than the ones in Greece itself.

South of the Bay of Naples with its resort islands of Capri (KAH-*pree*) and Ischia (ISS-*kee-yah*) winds the Amalfi (*ah*-MAHL-*fee*) Drive, a scenic road cut out of the cliffs that drop steeply to the sea below. Looking down you can see toy fishing villages set in blue coves. And above you are towns perched dizzily on the craggy heights.

The heel and toe of Italy are seldom visited by tourists because they are difficult to get to, and the climate is hot and dry. Sicily, too, is almost unbearably hot during the summer months, but its beauty and charm are great enough to lure visitors in spite of the heat. The racial strands that are interwoven throughout Italy are concentrated and intensified in the small island. Greeks, Phoenicians, Carthaginians, Romans, Goths, Byzantines, Saracens and Normans have left their stamp on the people as well as on the land. It is a powerful mixture, and the Italians of the mainland, colorful and volatile as they are, pale alongside the fiery Sicilians.

THE YOUNG NATION

We tend to think of Italy as one of the antique lands, but actually the nation was born in 1861, and the modern democratic republic in 1946. Through the many centuries of recorded history, there were few periods during which Italy was really unified. In the game of European power politics that followed the Renaissance, bits and pieces of this patchwork land were traded back and forth between other countries. Finally, after Napoleon united Italy under the Empire of France, some notion of national unity took root. After Napoleon's defeat, pieces of the peninsula were again parceled out—many of them to Austria. But Italy had at last begun to be a nation. It was at this time that she raised her three great patriotic sons—Cavour (*kah*-VOOR), Mazzini (*maht*-TSEE-*nee*) and the soldier-statesman Garibaldi (*gah-ree*-BAHL-*dee*). In 1861 the efforts of

13

these men resulted in the birth of a unified nation called Italy, with her first king, Victor Emmanuel II, a parliament and a capital, Turin. Rome and Venice had to be fought for separately, and within the next five years they, too, became part of the new nation.

After World War I, economic and political difficulties paved the way for the dark years of Mussolini's black-shirt dictatorship. The excesses of Fascism led, in turn, to the Second World War, which brought death to Mussolini, defeat and disorder to Italy. In 1946 the country voted against the monarchy that had been so spectacularly unsuccessful, and Italy became a democratic republic.

Italy's short history as a modern nation is far from splendid. But when we visit this young country we realize that Italy's greatness stems from the distant past. The country, as such, is less than a hundred years old, but for thousands of years the men who have inhabited this sunny land have ennobled it with their works. Etruscans, Romans, Venetians, the Florentines of the Renaissance—modern Italy is heir to them all. Their roads and bridges, their palaces and cathedrals, the paintings, sculpture and fabled cities of old—all these make a rich inheritance, and it is there, as well as in her natural beauty, that Italy's glory lies.

We will start our tour of Italy by following one of the many roads to Rome. Today the air lines, railroads and motor coaches all converge on Rome, carrying multitudes of visitors to this wondrous city. We will join them, and see for ourselves some of the treasures stored up here over the centuries.

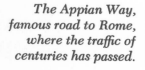

The Appian Way, famous road to Rome, where the traffic of centuries has passed.

let's travel in

CASTEL SANT' ANGELO: FORTRESS ON THE TIBER

FOR nearly thirty centuries, men have lived along these twisting banks of the Tiber, and the name of their great city echoes through the pages of history —Rome! Time has given the sun-warmed buildings a mellow glow, and the quiet river has held their reflection like this through the ages. From Vatican City behind the bridge, the dome of St. Peter's rises. In a city of domes and cupolas this perfect one, designed by Michelangelo (*my-kell-*AN-*jeh-low*), is the crowning landmark. The round building to the right is the Castel Sant' Angelo (*kahs-*TEHL *sahn* TAHN-*jeh-loh*), also known as Hadrian's Tomb. Many of the ancient structures in Rome had other buildings superimposed on them in later times. So it was with Hadrian's Tomb. Before the Emperor Hadrian died in 138 A.D., he had a large mausoleum built as a tomb for himself and succeeding emperors. It was sheathed in marble and decorated with columns and statues in the classical style. But in the third century, Emperor Aurelian decided that a fortress for the defense of his life would be more practical than a tomb. Later rulers used it as a prison and a castle. And later still it was connected to the Vatican by a secret passageway. In 1527, when Pope Clement VII was besieged in the Vatican by the forces of imperial Spain, he fled to Castel Sant' Angelo through this passageway, and the fortress kept him safe from the enemies of Rome.

The castle owes its name to a vision that Pope Gregory the Great had in 590. The Pope was leading a procession to pray for the deliverance of Rome from a terrible plague. Suddenly he saw the Archangel Michael sheathing his sword as a sign that the plague would end. To commemorate this event, a statue of the merciful archangel was placed on the top of the fortress. And much later two rows of white marble angels were added to the bridge that leads to the Castel Sant' Angelo. The five stories of the castle are open to the public and it is one of the most fascinating museums in Rome today. The city itself is a living museum, and a walk through its ancient streets is a visit to the past.

ROMAN FORUM: RUINS OF AN EMPIRE

THIS grassy plot with its rubble of stone and marble was once the hub of the whole civilized world. Rome had its beginnings in the eighth century B.C., and the legend of its founding is a famous one. Two wailing twin boys were abandoned on the Tiber shores, and a she-wolf raised them. One of the boys, Romulus (RAHM-*you-luss*), grew up with large ambitions. He took his plough and marked off a square plot around the Palatine (PAL-*ah-tyne*) Hill, which included the ground we are looking at now. This was the boundary of his original city. Whether or not Romulus and Remus really lived, tombs have been found beneath the Forum that date from that time, and traces of the earliest settlement were unearthed here.

This statue of Augustus, first emperor of Rome, addresses a senate that is no more.

Originally the Forum was the town market place. But as Rome grew, new and more beautiful buildings and temples were added. In this picture we see the curved walls of the Colosseum (*kahl-uh-*SEE-*um*) far in the background. The columns to our left are all that remain of an old Temple of Saturn. The senate house was not far from here, and the senators, realizing that even in wartime no one would dare to loot a holy place, cleverly stored the state money in the Temple of Saturn. In time it became the official treasury of Rome. The barbarians tore down much of the Forum, and the Romans themselves destroyed old buildings in order to build new ones.

18

OUTDOOR MARKET: LIVELY STREET SCENE

ONCE the Roman Forum was a bustling market place like this, alive with the citizens of ancient Rome. Now it is a quiet place of ruined grandeur, but the life of the city still pulses and throbs in the shabby back streets of Rome. The vitality of these Mediterranean people has endured through the centuries, and the daily business of living has been carried on with verve and enthusiasm while the fortunes of Rome rose and fell.

In this picture we get a glimpse of Italian city life in one of the poorer quarters. The old buildings, peeling and decayed, are crowded with families who overflow into the streets below. The Italians are warm and gregarious, and to them privacy would be chilling. They need to meet and mingle in the busy street, to gossip from their balconies and to market at open stalls like these, where buying the daily food becomes a sociable event. Family wash flaps from the windows, and whether the city is Rome, Naples, Milan—or even New York on Mulberry Street— the neighborhood acquires a colorful and "lived-in" look that is characteristically Italian.

You can tell, seeing the displays of brightly colored fruits and vegetables in this market, that they are favorite foods in Rome. And because the city is near the sea, fish is excellent here, too. Italian food is deservedly famous and the Roman cuisine is said to be the best in Italy. Egg noodles, called *fettuccine* (*feh-too-*CHEE-*neh*), served with butter and grated cheese, are the most popular *pasta* dish in Rome. The local peas, picked when they are still tiny and sweet, are a well-known delicacy. These and tender little artichokes cooked in a variety of imaginative ways could almost persuade one to become a vegetarian. Once you have tasted the delicious Roman fruits you will know why most meals here—even in the finest restaurants—end with a dessert of wild strawberries, figs, apples or oranges. In this sun-kissed land the most ordinary foods take on ambrosial flavors.

NEWS VENDOR IN ROME: COSMOPOLITAN ASSORTMENT

PILGRIMS and tourists pour into Rome, especially during the summer months, and their presence is reflected in the many magazines and periodicals for sale in different languages. Along the fashionable Via Veneto (VEE-*ah* VEH-*neh-toh*), lined with sidewalk cafés, the stroller can hear a veritable babel of foreign tongues. In the late morning the tables are filled with visitors from all over the world, and they sit in the warm sunshine, each with his paper or magazine, catching up on what's new in the Eternal City. Little newsstands like this one supply newspapers and magazines from all over the world. Or, if your Italian is up to it, there are the Roman daily newspapers.

The better morning newspapers in Rome devote their third page to articles of cultural interest—archaeology, art, history and scholarly subjects that make news in this ancient city. Page three is amusing, even to people who cannot read Italian, because the learned essays are inter-

Doney's, in the Via Veneto, is the gathering place for cosmopolitan Rome.

spersed with sprightly photographs of Italian movie actresses and girls in bathing suits. The men of this country take a lively and perpetual interest in pretty girls, and the elderly news vendor has stocked her stand with magazines that will also please the home-town trade.

THE COLOSSEUM: MAGNIFICENT MONUMENT

ONE of the pleasantest ways for a tourist to see Rome is in a leisurely *carrozza* (*kahr*-ROHT-*tsah*), or horse-drawn carriage. Although the traffic of Rome is made up of speeding cars and whizzing motor bikes, the city is best appreciated at a slow trot. In this picture an open carriage is waiting beneath the towering arches of the Colosseum. The enormous amphitheater was built in 72 A.D. to accommodate the Roman crowds who flocked there for games and public entertainment.

The Colosseum could seat 50,000 people, and they were a bloodthirsty audience. They sat shaded from the hot sun by cloth awnings and watched gladiators hack away at each other in mortal combat. The gladiators used to file past the emperor's box with the famous cry, "Hail Caesar! We who are about to die salute you!" The populace looked on unmoved when doomed prisoners—many of them condemned for belonging to the new Christian religion—were led out into the arena to be devoured by wild beasts.

The Colosseum today is a majestic ruin. The victorious barbarians who overran Rome ripped off the iron bands that held the giant blocks of stone together. Rome was desolated by pestilence and famine during the Dark Ages, and her great families deserted her. The fine buildings were abandoned to the wilderness, and weeds and thickets grew over the marble city. Later generations hammered away at the imperial monuments and used the marble for less distinguished structures. But though the glorious buildings of the Caesars fell into decay, Rome, the spiritual stronghold and capital of Christianity, survived and eventually prospered. Ancient pilgrims had a saying, "While stands the Colosseum, Rome shall stand; when falls the Colosseum, Rome shall fall; and when Rome falls—the world." The Colosseum still stands, though in ruins, and a modern city has taken the place of imperial Rome.

ST. PETER'S BASILICA: HEART OF THE VATICAN

O N THE west bank of the Tiber, across the river from the Rome of the Caesars, we stand now on the threshold of Vatican City. This is St. Peter's Square, and rising beyond it we see the largest church in Christendom. Two broadly curving colonnades spread out from the church around the square like embracing arms, and we are standing in the shadow of one of them, while our carriage waits for us. Michelangelo's dome rises behind the pillared portico from which the Pope addresses worshipers in the square and gives them his blessing. On holy days this vast area is a sea of humanity. The original church, built over the tomb of St. Peter in the fourth century, was in a state of near ruin in the sixteenth century. Pope Julius II decided to construct a new basilica and he called in the greatest architects and artists of the time, including Michelangelo and Raphael (RAFF-*ay-el*), whose masterpieces adorn the Vatican. The present basilica, their creation, was not completed for a hundred years.

You would never guess, seeing it from this angle, that the roof of the basilica just beneath the dome is like a small city. An elevator takes visitors to it, and there are photographers, small booths and shops, a place for mailing cards and the little houses of the men called Sanpietrini (SAHN-*pee-eh*-TREE-*nee*). The Sanpietrini have the privilege of doing all the repair work on the church and its dome, and it is said that, however high they climb, they never suffer dizziness. The Sanpietrini have another interesting function. There is one door on the extreme right of St. Peter's that is walled up except for the occasion of the Jubilee Year which falls every twenty-five years. It is a time of solemn and widespread pardon, and on Christmas Eve the Pope comes to open the Jubilee Gate. He knocks upon it with a golden hammer, and three times he says, "Open to me the gates of justice." Then the Sanpietrini demolish the stone partition in front of the door with their pikes. At the year's end the door on the right is blessed by the Pope and sealed up again by masons, to remain shut for another quarter century.

SWISS GUARDS:
LIVERY OF
THE RENAISSANCE

WHEN we are in Vatican City we are in the smallest state in the world. In 1929 the Church and the Italian government signed the Lateran Treaty, which granted sovereignty to the 108.7 acres of the Vatican. In this tiny state, completely walled off from the rest of Rome, the Pope holds absolute power—legislative, executive and judiciary. Only a thousand people live within the Vatican walls, but the Pope has spiritual jurisdiction over more than 400,000,000 souls all over the world.

The Swiss Guards, two of whom we see here, are perhaps the best known of the Vatican soldiery. Michelangelo designed their uniforms, and these young men are wearing their regular-duty costume. Though these guards look like characters from grand opera, they have a tradition of loyalty and valor. Several times the Swiss Guards have been called on to protect the Pope's life. When Pope Clement VII took refuge in Castel Sant' Angelo, it was the Swiss Guards who stood off the enemy until the Pope was safely inside the fortress. Every man of them lost his life. Each year now, on the anniversary of that day, the new recruits from Switzerland are sworn into the Guard in the courtyard of the Vatican.

There are only three gates through which you can enter Vatican City. The Swiss Guards are on duty at all three, and the Renaissance brilliance of their uniforms gives us a hint of the magnificence beyond the gates.

The square of St. Peter's on a rainy day gleams with a misty majesty.

HIGH ALTAR
OF ST. PETER'S:
SACRED MAGNIFICENCE

UNDER Michelangelo's perfect dome is the very heart of the Roman church. Here we see the high altar built above St. Peter's tomb. The bronze canopy with its twisted pillars and intricate carvings was the masterpiece of Bernini (*bare*-NEE-*nee*), one of the great sculptors and architects of the sixteenth century. In the flickering light of thousands of candles the marble and jasper and gold and mosaic have a warm radiance. Behind the altar stands the empty throne of St. Peter, and under the small canopy to the right, behind two lighted tapers, is the venerated bronze statue of St. Peter. On high occasions the statue wears a papal mitre and pontifical robes. It is believed to date from the earliest centuries of Christianity, and its right foot is worn smooth from the kisses of millions of devout worshipers. Under the lofty dome, mosaic letters six feet high spell out in Latin the words from Matthew:

"Thou Art Peter and upon This Rock
I Will Build My Church and I Will Give
Unto Thee the Keys to the Kingdom of Heaven."

Looking up at these words encircling the magnificent altar, we are reminded of the days when Peter himself was in Rome. Christians then had to worship in the dark tunnels of abandoned limestone quarries. Their dead were buried in the underground galleries, called catacombs, where the religious services were held in stealth. The pagan rulers of Rome mistrusted these meetings of people who refused to sacrifice to the old gods, so the Christians were hunted down and put to death, and Peter is believed to have been one of the many who perished in Nero's Circus. Devout followers came to gather up the remains of the martyrs and give them decent burial. Many years later Peter's remains were reinterred and placed beneath the old church that stood on the site of this basilica. Could he and his followers ever have dreamed that the crude stone altars of the catacombs would one day be replaced with this magnificence?

THE SPANISH STEPS: ROMAN RENDEZVOUS

ROME is a city of churches. Their spires and domes punctuate the skyline, and mornings begin with the ringing of bells from hundreds of towers. Here, we are looking up at the church of Trinità dei Monti (*tree-nee-*TAH *day* MOHN-*tee*), built at the time Columbus discovered America. It crowns the dramatic sweep of the Spanish Steps as they climb from the Piazza di Spagna (*pee-*AHTZ-*ah dee* SPAH-*nyah*) below. Every large city has a spot that is a favorite rendezvous for visitors as well as for its own citizens. In Rome, the popular meeting place is this piazza, or square, and the Spanish Steps rising from it.

Tourists are drawn to the square because the streets that converge here are lined with tempting shops. One street specializes in antiques, another in high fashion—which in Rome is very high indeed—and the fine handicrafts of the city. Though interesting shops are located on the square, what gives this place color and charm is the fact that it is the artists' quarter of the capital city of art. In the past it was at the Spanish Steps that artists and their models used to gather to exchange gossip with musicians and writers who were living in Rome. Wagner (VAHG-*ner*), Byron and Goethe (GEH-*teh*) found inspiration here. And the English poet Keats must have climbed these stairs many times on his way to the little house nearby where he lived and died.

The Spanish ambassador's residence used to be on the square, and that is what gave it its name. Actually the Spanish Steps were built as a gift from the French ambassador in the eighteenth century. In spring the flight of stairs has a cascade of pink and white azaleas spilling down either side. A fountain splashes in the square, inviting the footsore tourist to sit and rest awhile.

PIAZZA NAVONA: SPECTACLE OF LIGHTS

AT NIGHT this ancient city is at its most beautiful. Then the drama of its squares and fountains and the majesty of its ruined monuments are emphasized with artful illumination. Old buildings, scarred by time, can look shabby in the pitiless sunlight. But when darkness cloaks them and they become shadowy backgrounds for a statue or a column, Rome becomes dazzlingly young again.

Here, you see the Piazza Navona (*nah*-VOH-*nah*), one of the city's great squares, with its Fountain of the Rivers gleaming theatrically. In Roman times the Piazza Navona was a sports arena or stadium, which explains its oval shape. Chariots probably raced noisily where these fountains play. In the seventeenth century, Bernini, the architect who designed the colonnades and piazza in front of St. Peter's, beautified the square. He filled the space with three fountains, the central one representing the Río de la Plata, the Danube, Ganges and Nile rivers. Water and rock intermingle, and above them an Egyptian obelisk points skyward like a finger of light.

The fountains of Rome add their cool music to the sounds of the city, and at one of them, the Trevi (TREH-*vee*) Fountain, travelers throw coins into the blue-green water to ensure their return to this magical place.

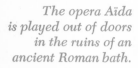

The opera Aïda is played out of doors in the ruins of an ancient Roman bath.

34

BAY OF NAPLES:
BLUE
ENCHANTMENT

THE silvery fountains of Rome, elegantly contrived, are a far cry from the vivid beauty of Naples curving around its warm blue bay. Only 143 miles from Rome, this southern city presents another and very different picture of Italy. From the time of its founding by ancient Greek navigators, until modern times, Naples has had a succession of rulers, drawn to the city by its mild climate and lovely site. The Neapolitans have known hardship under their numerous masters, but the people have maintained an exuberant vitality in spite of their poverty.

In Naples we are caught up in the gusty, noisy extravaganza of life in a south Italian town. Everyone seems to live out of doors, and snatches of laughter and song ring through the crowded streets. Naples is a city of music where everybody sings. Neapolitan melodies, like the people themselves, are gay on the surface, but with undertones of sadness. Many of the most famous ones extoll the loveliness of the city and its environs—"Santa Lucia" is a nostalgic tribute to the picturesque little harbor of that name, and "Come Back to Sorrento" tells of the seaside town near Naples. The city is noted for its more serious music, too. Its San Carlo Theater ranks with La Scala in Milan as one of the great opera houses of the world.

Viewed from a distance, Naples is a bright city whose houses climb the sunny hills that rise above the waterfront. In this picture we see a Neapolitan fisherman, descended from a long line of Mediterranean seafarers, mending his straw fishing traps on a quay. In the background, under an avenue of shade trees, is Naples' famous bayside promenade, and jutting out into the harbor we see a twelfth-century fortified castle. Slumbering in the blue distance, Mt. Vesuvius seems peaceful enough in this scene. Sometimes a little wisp of smoke hovers over the volcano —just enough to remind us that fires still burn deep within the barren cone, and that in the past its eruptions were deadly.

RUINS
OF POMPEII:
BURIED CITY

THE story of Pompeii (*pom-PAY*) is one of the most fascinating dramas of all time. This luxurious city was a thriving Roman colony lying about a mile from the foot of Mt. Vesuvius near the Bay of Naples. One August morning in the year 79 A.D. there was an earth-shaking explosion, and the top of the volcano split apart. A cloud of black smoke mushroomed into the sky, blotting out the sun. A dark rain of cinder and ashes fell, and birds plummeted to the ground, dead. At first there was only a light sifting of ash to fall on Pompeii. Many of Pompeii's 20,000 inhabitants fled towards Sorrento and out into the bay, but 2,000 stayed behind, thinking that they would be safe inside their houses. Fumes and the heavy hail of ashes killed them, and two days later, when the sun shone again and a harmless plume of smoke drifted up from Vesuvius, Pompeii was no more. Not until the eighteenth century did the city see the light of day again. Then, excavations uncovered a city of antiquity caught in the midst of its everyday life. Nowhere else is there such a record of the daily trivialities that added up to life under the Caesars. Rome with her majestic ruins can give us only the picture of civic institutions. But Pompeii lets us peek into the intimate lives of the citizens of this empire. Bread and roasted meats were found in ovens, and people were buried in volcanic ashes in their homes and on the streets. The ashes solidified, forming perfect molds of the men and women who lived nearly nineteen hundred years ago.

In this picture we are looking past the Temple of Apollo in the forum, and across the empty square towards Vesuvius with its white halo of smoke. Although Pompeii was a provincial town, it was a wealthy one, and we can get some feeling of its grace and elegance from the remains of these buildings in its forum. The private houses had great charm, with brightly painted walls whose pictures told a great deal about the customs of the time.

THE AMALFI COAST: VILLAGE BY THE SEA

FROM Sorrento, on the Bay of Naples, the coast arches southward in another curve that forms the Gulf of Salerno. Here the jagged mountains of the Apennines crowd right to the edge of the sea, and the combination of rocky slopes and brilliant blue water creates one of Italy's scenic marvels. Skirting the coast line for thirty miles, the Amalfi Drive winds above the sea, offering motorists a succession of dazzling views.

We are looking at Amalfi, an old village clinging to its terraced mountainside. The narrow beach is gay with umbrellas, awnings and the peppermint-striped bathhouses typical of Italian seashore resorts. Amalfi was not always the sparkling pleasure resort we see here. Fourteen hundred years ago it was a powerful maritime republic, the oldest in Italy, rivaling Pisa, Genoa and even Venice for dominion over the seas. The famous Tables of Amalfi, one of the earliest codifications of marine law, are on exhibit in the town's museum. They are worth seeing, but only on a rainy day.

When the sun shines on this southern coast, and the air is fragrant with the smell of citrus fruit, Amalfi seems happy to forget past greatness. Then, for its inhabitants as well as for visitors, the Italian motto holds true: *Dolce far niente* (DOLE-*cheh far* NYEN-*teh*)—"It is sweet to do nothing."

South Italian pottery is gaily decorated with cheerful peasant designs.

PLEASURE ISLAND: POOL AT ISCHIA

THE southern coast of Italy is adorned with a strand of bright villages and resorts strung along the Tyrrhenian Sea. But there are two gems set in the Bay of Naples that outshine the coastal towns. They are the islands of Capri and Ischia and they combine the special magic of island life with the luxury of resort hotels. In this picture we see one of the hotels at Ischia, with its swimming pool built out over the bay—a beautiful example of gilding the lily.

Ischia is the largest of Naples' islands, though it is only about twenty miles in circumference. It was formed by an underwater volcano, and its violent origin has given the island a wild and exciting beauty. The craggy rocks are bare in some places, but much of Ischia is green and lush, covered with fragrant pine woods, olive trees, and carefully ter-

This old peasant patriarch remembers the days when his island was a wild and lonely place.

raced gardens. The island has been a favorite resort for Italians because of its warm climate and beneficial thermal baths. The old volcano created a number of hot springs believed to be helpful in curing nearly every malady known to man. More and more foreign tourists are thronging to Ischia, but not just for the sake of the thermal baths. They find cure enough in the relaxation of a swimming pool, the sunshine and the healing beauty of this peaceful island.

42

FISHERMEN'S BAND: ISLE OF CAPRI

TIME was when Capri existed as a simple island Eden, the home of fishermen and peasants. It rose from the crinkled blue water about three miles from the mainland, picturesque and lonely, its beauty known only to a few. Within the past century, word of its scenic attractions spread, until finally the unspoiled island has become a tourist mecca receiving 60,000 visitors each year. They find much to admire in the five-and-a-half square miles of Capri.

The island thrusts up from the water in steep rocky cliffs. Its villages are hewn out of the stone at varying heights, and they enjoy spectacular views of the bay and the mainland. When your boat lands at Marina Grande (*mah*-REE-*nah* GRAHN-*deh*), you can take a funicular railway from the dock to the town above. The towns of Capri and Anacapri used to be connected by a flight of 784 steps, before a road was built to join them. Their sunny little squares are the only level places in these perpendicular villages, and they are usually crowded with tourists buying souvenirs at the shops or sitting at the outdoor cafés viewing the dazzling sights from behind sunglasses or cameras.

The Emperor Tiberius (*tie*-BEER-*ih-us*), who ruled Rome in the first century A.D., knew Capri, and he spent the last ten years of his life here. Ruins of a dozen of his splendid villas are scattered over the island. Today there are hotels on Capri that rival the Emperor's villas for elegance. But Capri is not all tourists—the native fishermen still live and work here, too. You can see them in the early morning far out on the flat blue water, waiting to haul in their nets. Or you can see them, as we do in this picture, set for an evening of music, dressed in Neapolitan costumes and playing the tarantella, their liveliest and most passionate folk dance. Behind this tarantella band, the sharp rocks jutting out of the water are the famous Faraglioni (*fah-rah*-LYOH-*nee*), landmarks of the enchanted Isle of Capri.

45

SARDINIA: THE UNKNOWN ISLAND

TOURISTS have discovered Capri, but the much larger island of Sardinia, lying 145 miles west of the Italian mainland, is still virtually unknown to visitors. It is a rugged and somewhat primitive land whose poverty is aggravated by summer drought and violent winds. Nevertheless, Sardinia is picturesque, and its villages, its herds of goats and sheep, the rough mountains and the Mediterranean beaches will someday attract their share of vacationers.

Here we see some fishermen readying their nets on the beach at Oristano (*oh-ree-*STAH*-noh*). Most fish nets in Italy are dyed this reddish color because the dye helps preserve them in the salt water. The fishermen will also tell you that a red net is less noticeable to the fish than a clean white one would be. Italians are not dedicated fishermen. They prefer working on the land, tending their vines and olive trees, or engaging in crafts and manufacture. When Italian fishermen do have to go to

A fisherman's shrine, framed with shells, stands near the shore of the treacherous sea.

sea, their boats never sail far from shore, and if they must take their nets out at night, they return to land the next morning.

These men are probably going out to catch a species of small tuna, the most plentiful and important product of Sardinian fishing. Sardines, whose name comes from this island, are also caught here and in the waters off Sicily.

SARDINIAN PEASANTS: LOCAL FIESTA

THE people of Sardinia have a long and dramatic history. Prehistoric caves and strange stone huts still exist here, and Carthaginians, Phoenicians, Greeks, Romans and Vandals once occupied this wind-swept island. In the eighteenth century the House of Savoy ruled Sardinia, and one of its monarchs, Victor Emmanuel II, became the first king of a united Italy. The costumes and traditions of the island reflect its fascinating background, and the people, swarthy and strong-featured, are products of the oldest Mediterranean strains.

The girls in this picture are dressed in the rich costumes of an earlier day. We see them in Cagliari (KAH-*lyah-ree*), the island capital, celebrating Sardinia's special holiday. On the first of May the patron saint of Cagliari is honored on the anniversary of his martyrdom with a procession to the beach where he was killed.

The procession starts in the city and slowly travels around the bay until it reaches the scene of the martyrdom eighteen miles away. Gaily decorated oxcarts carry dignitaries from every important village in Sardinia. The mayor of Cagliari, riding a white horse and dressed in top hat and cutaway, with a heavy silver chain around his neck, adds a touch of civic formality to the procession. Two musicians in brilliant costumes follow, playing Sardinian flutes, ancient and difficult instruments. Then comes the magnificent cart carrying the image of Saint Efisio (*eh*-FEE-*zyoh*), dressed in brocaded robes and jewels and glittering inside its glass-enclosed case. The clergy walks behind the saint's cart followed by two thousand peasants wearing the heavily embroidered costumes of their villages.

The procession stops for a festive dinner along the way and the saint's robes are exchanged for armor—supposedly to protect him from the bandits who once terrorized the countryside. The fiesta has been celebrated for over two hundred years, and every first of May the people of Sardinia rejoice in this colorful spectacle.

PAINTED WAGON:
SICILIAN
FOLK ART

SOUTHEAST of Sardinia and nearly touching the toe of the Italian boot lies Sicily, the largest island in the Mediterranean. Celebrated in myth and legend as the Island of the Sun and the Golden Island, Sicily is the inheritor of many great cultures. Within its six-hundred-mile circumference you can see Grecian temples and theaters, splendid Byzantine (*bih-*ZAN-*tin*) churches, Moorish cloisters, Norman castles (the Normans conquered Sicily six years before their conquest of England) and Renaissance palaces. Impressive as these buildings are, it is the vivid Sicilian folk art that delights the visitor and gives him the feeling of Sicily today.

The people of this fabled island are as colorful as the varied strands woven into their old civilization. Their costumes are brilliant, and Sicilian handicrafts show originality and inventiveness, whether in gaudy ceramics, glass inlay work, lace or richly patterned carpets. The

Sicilian puppets are nearly life-size and they recall the heroic tales of olden times.

donkey carts that one sees everywhere in Sicily are works of art. The one in this picture is typical, with its bright color and intricate design. Not for these proud and fiery people a pattern of flowers and curlicues! They paint their carts, and then in lavish detail they create elaborate historical scenes of kings and queens and great events. The history of Sicily comes to life on the gaily painted wagons used every day.

50

TEMPLE
AT AGRIGENTO:
MEMORY
OF GREECE

AN UNSUSPECTING traveler, whisked suddenly to the southern shore of Sicily, might easily believe he was in Greece. Actually Sicily was Greek long before it was Roman. In 735 B.C. the first Grecian settlement was founded near Taormina (*tah-or-*MEE-*nah*). Another city sprang up at Syracuse, and Agrigento (*ah-gree-*JEN-*toh*), where we are now, came into being in 581 B.C. For five hundred years these Hellenic communities thrived, and the coast of Sicily and parts of southern Italy are studded with classic Greek temples and theaters that are the inheritance of those centuries. When Rome colonized the rest of Italy with ruthless efficiency, these noble towns became second-rate provincial garrisons. Agrigento withered during the long Byzantine and Arab tenure, but today it is one of the chief cities of Sicily, with a population of about 40,000. The city is situated high on a hill with commanding views over the slope to the sea, where the Greek temples are scattered.

We are on the slope, which is carpeted with brilliant wild flowers. Boldly outlined against the sapphire sky is the Temple of Concord. This graceful little edifice has stood sharp and clear against the sky for an unbelievable 2,500 years! In the sixth century A.D. the Temple of Concord became a Christian church. Now it is a favorite spot with visitors, partly because it is the best-preserved Greek temple in Italy, and also because of its great beauty.

The fields of wild flowers near the Temple of Concord and the view of the sea below, glittering in the sunlight, are enough to attract tourists. But there is one oddity in the temple that people have gone out of their way to see. If you stand in just the right spot inside, two of the columns form the outline of a Greek vase against the sky. You feel you could reach out your hand to touch that giant vase of flawless heavenly blue.

TOWER
OF PISA:
TILTED
MASTERPIECE

THE building we are looking at now is probably the most famous tourist attraction in Italy. Certainly it has brought fame to the city of Pisa, which, in spite of former glories, would otherwise have been forgotten. Pisa was once a rich and powerful city of Tuscany, competing with Genoa for the supremacy of the Mediterranean. But nature has played strange tricks on the city, and one of the cruelest of them was to move the seacoast five miles farther out. For in the days of her greatness, around the twelfth century, the Pisan fleet was a force to be reckoned with, and the city controlled the islands of Corsica and Sardinia. It was then that the campanile, or bell tower, was built. The marble tower was certainly never intended to tip at such a crazy angle. When the first story had been built the ground probably shifted and settled. Nevertheless the building was completed. Measurements show that its angle of slant increases with the years. It was sixteen and one-half feet out of plumb last time it was measured, and engineers are studying ways and means to hold that line.

In a broad green field at the northwest corner of town, Pisa's most glorious buildings stand—the cathedral, the baptistery and the leaning tower. The beautiful buildings standing in this "meadow of miracles" have an interesting place in scientific history. Galileo (*gal-eh*-LEE-*oh*), the seventeenth-century astronomer and physicist, lived in Pisa. One day in the cathedral he noticed that the bronze lamp which hung from a great height was swinging back and forth. Its full swing took the same length of time regardless of the distance covered. From this observation Galileo formulated the principle of motion that governs a pendulum. The leaning tower was the scene of many of his experiments with gravity. Galileo would take skeptics up to the top of the bell tower and drop objects of varying weights to the ground below to show that they fell at the same rate of speed. Newton's apples, some years later, had a far less dramatic launching pad.

TUSCAN COUNTRYSIDE: TIMELESS LANDSCAPE

THE gently rolling hills of Tuscany have inspired Italy's greatest artists, and when we drive through that ageless countryside today we see it as it might have been hundreds of years ago. The teams of heavy white oxen have plodded across Italian fields as far back as the legendary times of Romulus. He is supposed to have put his yoke upon a white bull and heifer when he marked out the original boundaries of Rome. And the peasants of the neighboring province of Tuscany are still superstitious about white bullocks. They firmly believe that these great beasts bring them good luck. The Tuscan peasants have changed very little since the Middle Ages. They still cling to many of the old superstitions. Frequently you see a branch of a fir tree tied to the front door of a farmhouse. That is supposed to keep witches out. And there are charms and rigmaroles to perform over a newborn baby to assure that it does not have the evil eye.

Tuscany was settled about 800 B.C. by the Etruscans, who probably came from Asia Minor. Many of their ancient monuments and relics still remain. But it was in the Middle Ages and the Renaissance that the cities and villages of this tranquil land reached their full flowering of perfection. We see that perfection today in the harmony of rounded hills and pleasant valleys, olive groves and vineyards, and old walled towns drowsing behind a screen of tall cypress trees. We see it, too, in the beautiful Tuscan cities like Siena, Pisa, Arezzo (*ah*-RET-*so*) and Florence.

The rare beauty of the Italian land has served as inspiration for generations of great artists.

PONTE VECCHIO: OLD FLORENTINE BRIDGE

THE golden city of Florence is the brightest jewel of the Renaissance. It was here from the fourteenth to the sixteenth centuries that the sunburst of artistic and intellectual genius flashed through the darkness of the Middle Ages, heralding modern times. Dante (DAHN-*tay*), the great Italian poet; Leonardo da Vinci (*leh-oh-*NAHR*-doh dah* VEEN*-chee*), and Michelangelo, the artists; Galileo, the scientist; Machiavelli (*mah-kyah-*VEL*-lee*), the political philosopher, and the brilliant Renaissance architects—all added their luster to this city on the Arno River.

Florence is over two thousand years old, but age has only burnished its beauty to the golden glow we see here. Spanning the Arno on sturdy arches, the Ponte Vecchio (POHN*-teh* VEK*-kyoh*), or Old Bridge, is one of the famous landmarks of the city. A gallery runs across it, connecting the Pitti (PEE*-tee*) Palace with the Uffizi (*oo-*FEE*-tsee*), and art lovers can visit the magnificent collections in these two museums, using the Ponte Vecchio as a short cut.

The old bridge is lined with tiny shops—you can see them in this picture, clinging like barnacles to the sides of the Ponte Vecchio. Most of them are jewelers' shops where the exquisite work of Florentine goldsmiths and silversmiths is for sale. In the middle of the bridge there is a statue of the master craftsman of them all—Benvenuto Cellini (*behn-veh-*NOO*-toh cheh-*LEE*-nee*)—whose gold artifacts and madcap adventures brightened sixteenth-century Florence. It was at that time that Cosimo de Medici (KOH*-zee-moh day* MEH*-dee-chee*), Duke of Florence, made an improvement on the Ponte Vecchio. The shops that lined the bridge in those days belonged to the city's butchers, and Cosimo's artistic sensibilities were offended by the sight and smell of raw meat. Preferring to pass along an avenue of jewels and gold, he banned the butchers from the bridge and insisted that only jewelers could occupy the shops—as they have done ever since.

CHURCH OF SANTA CROCE: MAJESTIC SIMPLICITY

FLORENCE is an architect's dream of glorious buildings and churches, but the church of Santa Croce (sahn-*tah* kroh-*cheh*), which we see here, is more than an architectural masterpiece. It is a symbol of Italian genius to which Western culture owes so much. Enshrined within its marble walls are some of Italy's greatest sons—Michelangelo (whose body was smuggled out of Rome by the crafty Medici), Galileo, Machiavelli, Rossini (who composed *The Barber of Seville*), and scores of other famous men. Byron called this church the Westminster Abbey of Italy.

A large square in front of Santa Croce enables you to stand back and view its graceful symmetry from a distance. The rectangular designs in light and dark marble are typical of Florentine churches, and give them a sharpness and clarity that the years cannot dim. Santa Croce was built for the Franciscan monks in the thirteenth century, yet it looks fresh and modern today.

A statue of one of Italy's immortals stands in the square before the church. Dante, author of *The Divine Comedy*, and one of the ranking poets of the world, was banished from his native Florence because of his political activities. He is buried in the city of his exile, although by rights he should have had a place inside this Italian Pantheon. It was Dante who took the Florentine low-Latin idiom and used it for the first time in a literary work. His artistry established a new language—modern Italian.

This magnificent panel is from the Gate of Paradise, one of the bronze doors of the Baptistery in Florence.

FESTIVAL IN SIENA: MEDIEVAL PAGEANT

ITALY has been unified by its language, but otherwise each section and each city has traditions and customs that are distinctive. In Siena, another old Tuscan town, you see Italy as it must have been in the Middle Ages before it was touched by the glory of the Renaissance. Siena was an old Etruscan community when the Gauls took it over in 500 B.C., but it was not until the fourteenth century that it rose to the height of its power. Most of the buildings have a stern Gothic simplicity, and the city today retains its medieval character, looking much as it did when St. Catherine was born here. St. Catherine, who was responsible for bringing the Pope back to Rome from his exile in France, was one of the outstanding figures of the Middle Ages and her life has been the subject of many great paintings.

Siena itself inspired a famous school of painters, and looking at this picturesque festival we can understand why it has been a city beloved of artists. The colorful parade that we see here takes place every year on July 2 and August 16. Then the sleepy town comes to life; its ocher buildings are hung with flamboyant awnings; its citizens deck themselves out in the dramatic costumes of the sixteenth century. The festival called the *Palio* (PAH-*lyoh*) takes place in the Campo, Siena's large central square, and it has a fascinating history. For centuries Siena has been divided into districts known as *contrade* (kone-TRAH-*deh*), each intensely competitive with the others. Every year each district enters a horse and jockey in a race to be run around the great, shell-shaped Campo—you can see the mats hung against the buildings to protect horses and riders that might crash into them. The race is preceded by the parade we see here, with citizens of every *contrada* dressed in the special colors of their district. Later, after being blessed in the parish churches, the horses will gallop madly around the Campo. The winner will be awarded a banner, or *palio*, and the victorious district will go joyously wild with true Italian fervor.

COLUMBUS' BIRTHPLACE: PORT OF GENOA

ITALY'S busiest seaport lies in the curve of shore at the northwest of the Italian boot top. The narrow crescent of land hemmed between mountains and the sea is called Liguria (*lih-GOO-ree-ah*). With Genoa at the center, this curving shelf of land forms the Italian Riviera, a garland of beautiful little towns strung along the sea. San Remo (*sahn REH-moh*), Camogli (*kah-MOH-lyee*), Portofino (*por-toh-FEE-noh*) and Rapallo (*rah-PAHL-oh*) are just a few of the resorts and fishing villages that have made this stretch of seacoast a favorite with vacationers from every country. Genoa, however, is strictly business. It has always been a great maritime center, sending its ships out to the far corners of the world. When Christopher Columbus was born here, the son of a weaver, Genoa was undergoing one of her periods of internal struggle. It was an inauspicious time to try to raise money for a venture such as Columbus had in mind. To his native city's everlasting loss, Columbus went to Spain with his project and finally got help there. The rest is history.

The plain little house where Columbus was born has been preserved by the city. A Latin inscription tells us that "Here Christopher Columbus Spent his Childhood and Early Youth." Just behind the ivy-covered house we see the Soprana Gate, part of the medieval wall that was hastily thrown up around the city in 1155 to defend it from attack. This picturesque city climbs from the sea up the lower slopes of the Apennines, and consequently it is built on several levels. At the lowest level is the port, crowded, noisy, smelly, choked with the masts and funnels of hundreds of ships flying the flags of every nation. The middle level of the town has old palaces, banks, hotels and some new skyscrapers. Still higher, and reached by elevators and funiculars, the rim of hills that encloses the city offers a magnificent view over rooftops and harbor. Looking down over Genoa you can understand why she was called *La Superba*.

65

ELEGANT ARCADE: SHOPPING IN MILAN

MILAN conceals its two-thousand-year history beneath the bustling modernity of an industrial metropolis. This northern city, the second largest in Italy, is the most important commercial center in the country, but its preoccupation with business tends to make us lose sight of its artistic achievements. Milan has treasures to rival those of Rome and Florence, among them the masterpiece of Leonardo da Vinci—*The Last Supper*—and an opera house, La Scala, whose peerless productions have made musical history.

Until the period between the two World Wars, Milan was the largest city in Italy, and for centuries it has been a powerful political force in the struggle for Italian independence. This was the city that first gave support to Mussolini, but it later repudiated him savagely, and in one of Milan's little squares the dictator, who had been captured and killed, was displayed to an angry public.

Today the city has repaired the severe damage done by five years of wartime bombardment. Its citizens are friendly and warmhearted, gracious hosts to visiting Italians and foreigners who come to Milan for business or pleasure. In this picture we see the enormous Victor Emmanuel Arcade, or *Galleria* (*gahl-leh*-REE-*ah*), a glass-roofed street of shops and restaurants where Milan entertains its visitors. There are similar *gallerias* in Naples, Rome and Genoa, but this one is by far the most imposing. Rain or shine, night and day, the domed glass roof echoes to the clatter of footsteps and the noisy gaiety of promenading crowds. At the café tables people watch the passing parade while sipping a Milanese apéritif called Campari (*kahm*-PAH-*ree*), or enjoying coffee and the pastry for which Milan is renowned. The shops alone would make the *Galleria* a must on any tourist's itinerary, for they offer a selection of all the wonderful merchandise of the entire country. Travelers would do well to save their shopping for this convenient center, instead of burdening themselves with souvenirs at every stage of their trip.

MOUNTAIN PEOPLE: ITALIAN ALPS

HIGH in an Alpine valley near the Swiss and Austrian borders we see a Tirolese woman and her little girl burdened with hay from the mountainside. These hardy people live at an altitude of over five thousand feet, with spectacular peaks towering still higher above the little valleys. The Tirol (*tih*-ROHL) is vastly different from any other section of Italy, not only because of its mountain grandeur, but also because its people are Germanic rather than Italian. This region only became part of Italy in 1918, and many of its inhabitants still speak a variety of German. The flag they live under seems to be far less important than the splendor of the Alpine landscape that has molded their way of life.

In this picture we see the road to the Stelvio (STEL-*vyoh*) Pass near the village of Trafoi (*trah*-FOY). The road climbs from valley to valley in a series of breath-taking hairpin bends, until it reaches the Pass at the Swiss border, more than nine thousand feet above sea level—the highest in Europe. Every season of the year has its special attractions in the Italian Tirol. The green and blossoming valleys of spring and summer give way to the sparkling white landscapes of winter, when ski enthusiasts race down Alpine slopes. At any time, visitors can count on magnificent scenery, and the traditional hospitality of these mountain people.

A cable car carries skiers to the mountain slopes high above Cortina.

REGATTA:
LAKE GARDA

ITALY is a land of lovely playgrounds, and its northern lakes, stretching down from the Alps like long, blue fingers, are famous for their resorts. Here, at Lake Garda, we glimpse the majesty of mountains silhouetted against a clear sky, forming a striking backdrop for the sapphire water. The pleasures of sailing must be increased a hundredfold in such a setting, and the losers of this race need only lift up their eyes unto the hills for consolation.

Lake Garda is the largest lake in Italy, and though it is narrow, it measures about 32 miles from north to south. Sheltered between the Alps and the Po Valley, Garda enjoys a semitropical climate that is pleasant even in February and March. The summer months are glorious, as the heat is nearly always tempered by a lake breeze.

In the old days, palatial villas dotted the hills around the Italian lakes, their formal gardens vying with the natural beauty around them. Now, many of the great private villas have been turned into hotels, and more modest summer homes crowd the lake shores. White steamers crisscross the blue water, carrying throngs of sight-seers. Sounds of music and laughter drift across the lake, and the fragrance of oleanders, ripening grapes, oranges and lemons hangs in the air. Roads have been blasted out of the mountainsides skirting the lake, and as you travel along them, it is possible to stop at an open-air restaurant and dine at the lapping water's edge.

Poets have sung of Lake Garda's beauty in many ages and many languages—Vergil and Horace in Latin, Goethe in German, Dante in Italian and Tennyson in English. Yet each generation of visitors feels that it has discovered this place, and Lake Garda has accommodated itself to changing times and tastes without losing one iota of its charm.

THE
GRAND CANAL:
VENETIAN
THOROUGHFARE

THE white sails on Lake Garda have been replaced in this scene by the gondolas (GAHN-*doh-luhs*) of Venice, and we have come at last to the queen city of the Adriatic. There is no other place in the world like Venice, which seems to rise out of the water miraculously on either side of the Grand Canal. The city floats on more than a hundred small islands which are lashed together by bridges. Its streets are canals, the traffic is made up of boats, and the old buildings that stand at the water's edge shimmer with reflections from every ripple.

In the beginning, the islands sprinkled over this placid lagoon were inhabited by poor and simple fishermen. But when the barbarian Huns swept down from the north in the fifth century, refugees from the mainland sought shelter in the marshes and on the islets. Eventually the isolated community in the lagoon became independent. It had its own government under a Doge (DOHJ), and for a while it was one of the richest, most powerful cities in the world.

In the days when Venice ruled the Adriatic and the eastern Mediterranean, there was a brilliant ceremony performed every year on Ascension Day. The Doge, dressed as a magnificent bridegroom, was rowed out to the end of the lagoon near the Lido. There he cast a ring into the sea, and as it flashed into the blue waters, the Doge married the Adriatic symbolically with this pledge, "We wed thee, oh our sea, in sign of true and perpetual dominion." Venice was the gateway to the East until the end of the fifteenth century. Her fleet brought back the riches of the world, and the city was decked out in Oriental splendor. The palaces on the left are typical of the elegant Venetian homes built by the merchants and princes of the Renaissance. The striped poles in front of them are moorings for gondolas and other boats. If you are in a hurry—and in Venice you shouldn't be—you can sail the canals in a *vaporetto* (*vah-poh-*RET-*toh*), a little steam launch like the ones on the right in this picture. They are not as colorful as the gondolas, but then the fare is only a dime.

73

BASILICA
OF ST. MARK:
TREASURE HOUSE
OF VENICE

THE center of Venetian life, drawing crowds to it like a magnet, is the great square of St. Mark. Cafés surrounding the square have hundreds of little chairs and tables set out on the broad pavement. Thousands of pigeons gather here to be fed by generous tourists. People stroll through the arcades of the palaces along one side of St. Mark's Square, which has been called "the most beautiful room in Europe." In this outdoor "room" there is a band concert every Saturday and Sunday evening. And from the Clock Tower the hours are rung on a bronze bell. But of all the marvels and delights that captivate the visitor to the square none can compare with the splendor of the Byzantine church we are looking at now.

When the remains of St. Mark were brought to Venice from Alexandria in the ninth century, a small church was built here as a final resting place. It was rebuilt in the eleventh century, and further additions were made to it until about eighty years ago. The wealth and taste and imagination that were characteristic of Venice in her centuries of greatness are reflected in this building. It was a law of the republic that any Venetian engaged in trade with the East must bring back some treasure for the adornment of St. Mark's. Pillars were taken from Greek temples, bronzes from Rome; alabaster, enamel, gold work, agate, porphyry were taken from buildings in the East and on the mainland. The most glorious mosaic work adorns the façade of the basilica. Just above the central arch four colossal bronze horses prance. They were probably triumphal steeds from a Greek or Roman victory arch, taken to Byzantium, and brought from there by a Venetian Doge to decorate St. Mark's. Napoleon cast a jealous eye at them and had them sent to Paris, but they came back to Venice. Here they belong, looking down at the busy square, their polished bronze glinting in the sun.

ARTISTRY IN GLASS: ISLAND OF MURANO

OUT in the flat blue wastes of the lagoon you can visit the satellite islands of the Queen of the Adriatic. There is Burano (*boo-*RAH*-noh*), beloved of painters and famous for its lace; picturesque Torcello (*tor-*CHEL*-loh*), the mother island of Venice, where the first harried mainlanders sought refuge from the barbarians. Most interesting of all is Murano (*moo-*RAH*-noh*), where the exquisite Venetian glass is made. Nearly all of Murano's inhabitants earn their living from glassware, which has been manufactured on the island for hundreds of years. In this shop you can see the fragile masterpieces of the Murano artists.

The Venetians were the first glassmakers to produce a clear, crystalline glass. They guarded their secret jealously, and no craftsman was permitted to leave Venice and work elsewhere or to teach his trade to a non-Venetian. Several hundred years ago one of the Doges became alarmed at the fire hazard created by the glassmakers in Venice. Their glass had to be heated to a liquid state before it was molded or blown, and the great open hearths were dangerous. So the entire industry was moved to Murano, and there the furnaces have glowed steadily through the years. When you buy these airy delicacies of Venetian glass and bring them home with you, they seem to hold all the shimmering colors of Venice and the lovely Adriatic.

The art of Venetian glass has come down through the centuries to this skilled craftsman.

ROMANTIC RIDE:
FLOATING
IN A GONDOLA

THE classic way to see Venice is, of course, in a gondola. These slim, black-lacquered craft glide past the sights of the romantic city, giving their passengers the feeling of moving through a dream. Here we see a straw-hatted gondolier silhouetted against one of the splendid Venetian palaces—the House of Gold. Built as a private residence five hundred years ago, the *Ca' d'Oro* (*kah* DOH-*roh*), as the Venetians call it, was so named because originally its lacy façade was gilded. Today it is an art museum, but the masterpieces within its marble walls can scarcely match the beauty of the city that surrounds it.

This is true, on a larger scale, of the whole lovely country of Italy. While it is a fabulous repository for artistic and historical treasures, the land itself is of such surpassing beauty that art must bow to nature. The Italian people, with their operatic sense of drama and color, accentuate the vivid charm of their country. The pleasures of life are nowhere more apparent than in Italy, and no one can be here for long without having his senses and feelings deeply engaged. The visitor to this country may be impressed at first with its reminders of past splendors, but he soon comes to love the vitality and warmth of the living present. And when he leaves, he takes more than a memory with him. With Robert Browning he can say:

"*Open my heart, and you will see
    Graved inside of it, 'Italy'.*"

*A sunny beauty,
a scenic background—
this is the final
remembrance of Italy.*

SOME FAMOUS DATES IN ITALIAN HISTORY

753 or 754 B.C.	*Legendary founding of Rome by Romulus on the banks of the Tiber.*
264-146 B.C.	*Period of the three Punic Wars with Carthage. Hannibal crosses the Alps into Italy during Second Punic War.*
60 B.C.	*The first triumvirate of Caesar, Pompey and Crassus formed to govern the rapidly expanding Roman Empire.*
44 B.C.	*Assassination of the newly appointed dictator of Rome, Julius Caesar. Octavian, later called Augustus, wins subsequent battle for power.*
96-180 A.D.	*Growth of the Roman Empire. The Golden Age of art, literature and Roman law.*
313	*Constantine the Great is the first Roman emperor to be converted to Christianity. Ten years later he moves the capital of the Roman Empire to Constantinople and divides the civilized world into the Eastern and Western Empires.*
476	*The fall of the Roman Empire.*
493-555	*Barbarian Ostrogoths rule Italy.*
555	*Italy under Byzantine government, ruled from Constantinople.*
590	*Gregory, bishop of Rome, becomes the first Pope of the Catholic world, establishes the ecclesiastical supremacy of Rome.*
800	*Charlemagne crowned Emperor of the West on Christmas Day.*
13th-15th centuries	*Guelph and Ghibelline struggles; Papalist and Imperialist parties fight for control of the powerful city-states.*
1494-1706	*French and Spanish invasions.*
1713-1796	*Italy under Austrian influence.*
1796-1814	*Napoleon in Italy. First campaigns in 1796. Napoleon's brother, Joseph Bonaparte, crowned King of Naples, 1806. Restoration in Italy, 1814.*
1848-1861	*Revolutionary wars. Conquest of Southern Italy by Garibaldi in 1859-1860, coupled with political actions of Count Camillo Cavour in Rome, brings about unification of the Italian city-states.*
1861	*Victor Emmanuel II proclaimed King of united Italy.*
1915-1918	*World War I. Italy first chooses neutrality because of alliances with Germany and Austria. Enters war in 1915 on the side of the Allies.*
1922	*Mussolini's "march on Rome."*
1929	*Lateran Treaty signed under Mussolini's regime. Allows the existence of independent Vatican City state over which the pope exercises temporal rule.*
1935-1936	*Italians invade Abyssinia.*
1940-1945	*World War II. Italy is one of the Axis powers. Rome falls to the Allies in 1944.*
1946	*Republic of Italy established.*
1948	*Constitution is ratified. Recognizes Roman Catholicism as the state religion, incorporates the Lateran Treaty.*

SOME FAMOUS NAMES IN ITALIAN HISTORY

JULIUS CAESAR (100-44 B.C.)—*Roman soldier-statesman.*

AUGUSTUS CAESAR (63 B.C.-14 A.D.)—*First Emperor of Rome. United the Roman Empire after the decisive Battle of Actium against Mark Antony in 31 B.C. Established constitution; declared Emperor in 27 B.C.*

VERGIL (70-19 B.C.)—*National poet of ancient Rome. Traced the legendary history of the Empire in the great epic,* The Aeneid.

ST. AUGUSTINE (354-430)—*Great Christian bishop and the first powerful voice of early Christian philosophy.*

ST. FRANCIS OF ASSISI (1182-1226)—*Catholic friar; founded the confraternity of Franciscans in 1209. Canonized in 1228 by Pope Gregory IX.*

ST. THOMAS AQUINAS (1225?-1274)—*Dominican monk. Became leading Scholastic philosopher of the Middle Ages.*

MARCO POLO (1254?-1324?)—*Venetian traveler and author. Early journeys to China and the court of Kublai Khan initiated interest in exploration and the seeking of new trade routes.*

DANTE ALIGHIERI (1265-1321)—*Greatest poet of the Italian Renaissance; author of the* Divine Comedy.

PETRARCH (1304-1374)—*Petrarchan poems mark beginning of Renaissance literature. Originator of new form and new literary language.*

GIOVANNI BOCCACCIO (1313-1375)—*Italian author, humanist, poet.*

LORENZO GHIBERTI (1378-1455)—*Florentine sculptor. Commissioned to design and execute the bronze doors of the Baptistery of Florence.*

GIOVANNI BELLINI (1430?-1516)—*Master of the Venetian school of Renaissance art; teacher of Titian.*

CHRISTOPHER COLUMBUS (1451-1506)—*Genoese discoverer of the New World.*

LEONARDO DA VINCI (1452-1519)—*Florentine painter, sculptor, architect, scientist, inventor and engineer. Among his many artistic contributions are the* Last Supper *and the* Mona Lisa.

NICCOLÒ MACHIAVELLI (1469-1527)—*Statesman and political theorist. Author of* The Prince. *His concept of man as a political being is basis of modern politics.*

MICHELANGELO BUONARROTI (1475-1564)—*Leading artist of the Florentine school. Florence's statue of the young* David, *the Sistine Chapel ceiling in Rome and the* Pietà *are a few of the works of this prolific artist.*

THE MEDICI—*One of the powerful families of Renaissance Italy; masters of Florence during the ascendancy of the city-state. Leaders of the Church (Pope Clement VII, 1478-1534); patrons of the arts.*

TITIAN (1477-1576)—*Venetian painter, pupil of Bellini. His magnificent paintings decorate many of the churches and museums of Italy.*

RAPHAEL (1483-1520)—*Renaissance painter famous for his renditions of the Madonna and Child.*

GIUSEPPE GARIBALDI (1807-1882)—*Patriot and revolutionary leader. With Cavour, Crispi and others, he succeeded in uniting the city-states into a nation.*

CAMILLO BENSO DI CAVOUR (1810-1861)—*Greatest Italian statesman. Father of modern Italy.*

GIUSEPPE VERDI (1813-1901)—*Operatic composer;* Rigoletto, La Forza del Destino, Il Trovatore *made his name famous the world over.*

GIACOMO PUCCINI (1858-1924)—*Another of Italy's contributors to the opera. Composer of* Manon Lescaut, La Bohème, Tosca, Madame Butterfly.

AMADEO MODIGLIANI (1884-1920)—*Painter and sculptor. One of the exponents of revolutionary art movements in Paris with Picasso, Utrillo, Matisse.*

SOME ITALIAN WORDS AND PHRASES

Here is a list of words and phrases that you might be likely to use when traveling in Italy. The words are written in simple phonetics for the Italian pronunciation, with accented syllable in small capitals.

Yes No	Si (*see*) No (*noh*)
Perhaps	Forse (FOHR-*seh*)
Thanks (very much)	Grazie (tanto) (GRAH-*tsyeh*) (TAHN-*toh*)
Please	Per favore (*pehr fah-*VOH-*reh*)
Excuse me	Mi scusi (*mee* SKOO-*zee*)
What do you wish?	Che cosa vuole (*keh* KOH-*sah* VWOH-*leh*)
Who? Why?	Chi (*kee*) Perchè (*pehr-*KEH)
When? How long?	Quando (KWAHN-*doh*) Quanto tempo (KWAHN-*toh* TEM-*poh*)
Where? How far?	Dove (DOH-*veh*) A che distanze (*ah keh dis-*TAHNT-*sah*)
How much?	Quanto (KWAHN-*toh*)
Do you speak English?	Parla inglese (PAHR-*lah een-*GLEH-*seh*)
I do not understand.	Non capisco (*nohn kah-*PEE-*skoh*)
How do you say . . . ?	Como si dice . . . (KOH-*meh see* DEE-*cheh*)
Hello Goodbye	Ciao (CHAH-*oo*) Addio (*ahd-*DEE-*oh*)
I'll be seeing you.	Arrivederci (*ahr-ree-veh-*DEHR-*chee*)
The washroom	Il gabinetto (*eel gah-bee-*NET-*toh*)
Ladies' Men's	Per donne (*pehr* DOHN-*neh*) Per uomini (*pehr* WOH-*mee-nee*)
Hotel Room	Albergo (*ahl-*BEHR-*goh*) Camera (KAH-*meh-rah*)
Airplane Airport	L'aereo (*lah-*EH-*reh-oh*) L'aeroporte (*lah-eh-roh-*POHR-*teh*)
Train Station	Il treno (*eel* TREH-*noh*) La stazione ferroviaria (*lah stah-*TSYOH-*neh fehr-roh-vee-*AH-*ryah*)
Baggage Customs	Bagaglio (*bah-*GAH-*lyoh*) Dogana (*doh-*GAH-*nah*)

DAYS OF THE WEEK

Monday	Lunedì (*loo-neh-*DEE)
Tuesday	Martedì (*mahr-teh-*DEE)
Wednesday	Mercoledì (*mehr-koh-leh-*DEE)
Thursday	Giovedì (*joh-veh-*DEE)
Friday	Venerdì (*veh-nehr-*DEE)
Saturday	Sabato (SAH-*bah-toh*)
Sunday	Domenica (*doh-*MEH-*nee-kah*)
Day Night	Il giorno (*eel* JOHR-*noh*) La notte (*lah* NOHT-*teh*)
Yesterday Tomorrow	Ieri (YEH-*ree*) Domani (*doh-*MAH-*nee*)
Year	L'anno (LAHN-*noh*)

NUMBERS

One	uno (OO-*noh*)	Seven	sette (SET-*teh*)
Two	due (DOO-*eh*)	Eight	otto (OHT-*toh*)
Three	tre (*treh*)	Nine	nove (NOH-*veh*)
Four	quattro (KWAHT-*troh*)	Ten	dieci (DYEH-*chee*)
Five	cinque (CHEEN-*kweh*)	One hundred	cento (CHEHN-*toh*)
Six	sei (SEH-*ee*)	One thousand	mille (MEEL-*leh*)

INDEX